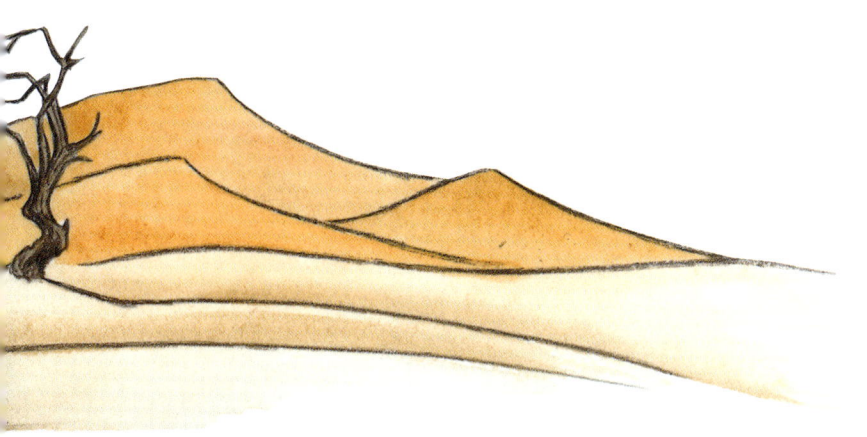

The Four Elements
EARTH

Text by Connor Dayton
Illustrations by Cecco Mariniello

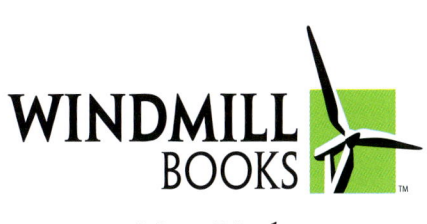

New York

Published in 2015 by Windmill Books, An Imprint of Rosen Publishing
29 East 21st Street, New York, NY 10010

Copyright © 2015 by Windmill Books, An Imprint of Rosen Publishing

All rights reserved. No part of this book may be reproduced in any form without permission in writing from the publisher, except by a reviewer.

Illustrations by Cecco Mariniello
Computer graphics by Roberto Simoni

Photo Credits: p. 8 cpphotoimages/Shutterstock.com; pp. 8–9 Pakhnyushcha/Shutterstock.com; p. 9 LiliGraphie/Shutterstock.com; p. 17 (left) Nataly Lukhanina/Shutterstock.com; p. 17 (right) valzan/Shutterstock.com; p. 18 Anton Petrus/Shutterstock.com; p. 21 Vladimir Sazonov/Shutterstock.com; p. 22 eyeidea/Shutterstock.com; p. 27 Aleks49/Shutterstock.com.

Library of Congress Cataloging-in-Publication Data

Dayton, Connor.
Earth / by Connor Dayton.
    pages cm. — (The four elements)
Includes index.
ISBN 978-1-4777-9276-6 (library binding) — ISBN 978-1-4777-9273-5 (pbk.) — ISBN 978-1-4777-9274-2 (6-pack)
1. Geology—Juvenile literature. 2. Earth (Planet)—Juvenile literature. 3. Four elements (Philosophy)—Juvenile literature. I. Title.
QE29.D39 2015
551—dc23
                                    2013050481

Manufactured in the United States of America

CPSIA Compliance Information: Batch # BW14WM: For Further Information contact Windmill Books, New York, New York at 1-866-478-0556
Windmill Books wishes to thank AD Books for original creation of content in this book.

Contents

Introduction	6
Feet on the Ground	8
Living in the Earth	10
Land and Sea	12
The Nourishing Earth	14
Rocky Earth	16
Grinding up Rocks	18
What Rocks Tell Us	20
Treasures Underground	22
The Restless Earth	24
Using Earth	26
A Delicate Balance	28
Glossary	30
Further Reading	31
Index	32
Websites	32

The Four Elements

In the ancient world, most people thought the world was made of four **elements**. These elements were water, fire, air, and earth.

Today, we know much more about what the world is made of. We still use the term element for these materials. Scientists have found 92 elements on Earth, while even more exist in space.

This series will teach you about the real science behind the four original elements. None of them are thought of as elements today, but they are all important to our world.

Feet on the Ground

Scientists learn about the world by **observation**. Observation is the act of looking at and noticing something. You can try this yourself! Walk around barefoot in a park, at a beach, or inside your home.

In your home, you might feel cold tile floors and soft carpets. Outside, the grass may feel ticklish. Cement will feel rough. Use your sense of touch to see how different the surface of the planet is.

Living in the Earth

When you see a flower, it looks like the whole plant is above ground. Actually, plants have **roots** underground. Roots take **nutrients** and water out of soil to help plants live and grow.

Animals also live inside the earth. For example, earthworms make homes just below the surface. Mice come to the surface to find food, but they spend much of the time in burrows. Burrows are underground holes and tunnels.

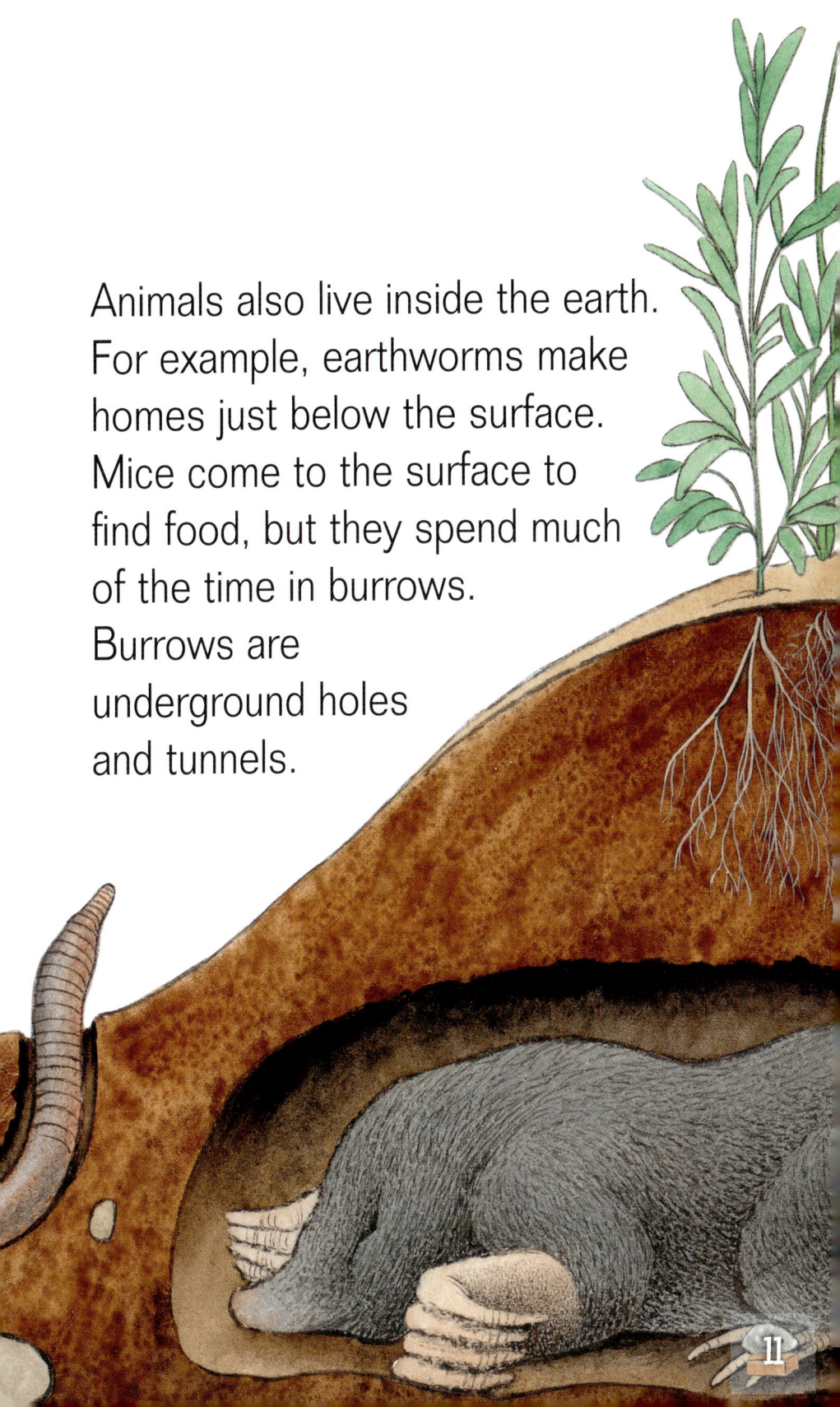

Land and Sea

70 percent of Earth's surface is water. This includes rivers, lakes, and oceans. Even though water covers most of the Earth, it is not part of the Earth's **crust**. The crust is the outer layer of a planet. Oceans and lakes sit on top of the crust.

70%

The other 30 percent of the Earth's surface is land. This land includes all deserts, mountains, forests, cities, and countryside. Only a third of this land is fit for humans to live on. This means that all of the people in the whole world live in only 10 percent of the Earth's surface!

The Nourishing Earth

Growing food is an important thing that humans must do to survive. Farmers have planted seeds in soil to grow food for thousands of years. Farmers first grew food in

areas near rivers. The rivers left rich soil behind after flooding. And they provided water the plants needed. Some ancient farmers carved flat fields, called terraces, out of hillsides.

Rocky Earth

If you dig underneath any part of the Earth's surface, you will eventually hit the rock layer of the earth's crust.

In some areas of Earth, there are miles of soil, dead plants, and sand above the rock layer. In other areas, the rock is just a few feet or inches under the ground.

Not all rock is the same. Most rocks, like granite and basalt, don't let light through. Rocks of this type make up most of the crust. Diamonds, rubies, and emeralds, are examples of clear and beautifully-colored rocks, called gems. These rocks, which are hard to find, are often made into jewelry.

Grinding up Rocks

All of the small rocks, silt, and sand that you see today are rocks that have been crumbled up over millions of years. Rivers **erode**, or break down, rocks as water runs over them. At the edge of an ocean, the waves break down rocks and reefs along the shore until all that's left is a sandy beach! Rock erosion also happens when the wind blows against rocks for millions of years.

What Rocks Tell Us

Fossils are the hardened remains of a dead animal or plant. There are fossils deep inside Earth's rock formations. These layers used to be on the Earth's surface.

The fossils in these layers tell us what kinds of animals and plants lived on Earth when that layer was at the Earth's surface. Scientists have even found human fossils from nearly 200,000 years ago!

Treasures Underground

There are all kinds of valuable and important things underneath the Earth's surface. We get our oil, coal, diamonds, and more from deep inside the Earth's crust.

Giant, deep, manmade holes in the ground from which people take these materials are called **mines**.

The Restless Earth

Humans cannot go to the center of the Earth. However, we can still learn a lot about what happens there.

For example, volcanoes send hot **lava** from deep within the Earth to the surface. Scientists study the lava to learn about what makes up the layers below the crust.

Land on Earth's surface also moves. We know this for several reasons. For example, some of the same **species** of animals live on different continents, separated by water. This means that these continents must have been connected at some point. This slow process is called continental drift.

Using Earth

Thousands of years ago, humans discovered that they could make things out of certain materials found on Earth. They turned sand and clay into dishes, containers, and pots.

These inventions helped humans live better lives. They could now store the food they made. People also made artwork out of these same materials.

People even built houses and other buildings out of mud and clay. Even today, bricks used to build houses are made from ground-up rocks and other materials from the ground. So, people have always used materials from the Earth to make our lives better.

A Delicate Balance

We use the Earth to make our lives better, but sometimes we harm it. While coal mines give us coal to use for energy, we have to burn the coal to use it. This **pollutes** the air. Also, when farmers use the same crops in the same land for many years, the soil loses many of its nutrients.

Another problem is deforestation. This is when people cut down many trees to clear an area for farming or building. Trees help make oxygen, which people need to breathe.

Luckily, there are many people around the world who work to protect Earth. Maybe you will grow up to help keep Earth a safe, healthy place!

Glossary

crust (KRUST) The outer, or top, layer of a planet.

elements (EH-luh-ments) The basic things of which all other things are made.

erode (ih-ROHD) To be worn away slowly.

fossils (FO-sulz) The hardened remains of dead animals or plants.

lava (LAH-vuh) Hot, melted rock that comes out of a volcano.

mines (MYNZ) Pits or underground tunnels from which stones are taken.

nutrients (NOO-tree-ents) Food that a living thing needs to live and grow.

observation (ahb-ser-VAY-shun) The act of looking at or noticing something.

pollutes (puh-LOOTS) Hurts with certain kinds of bad matter.

roots (ROOTS) The parts of plants or trees that are underground.

species (SPEE-sheez) One kind of living thing. All people are one species.

Further Reading

Appleby, Alex. *Happy Earth Day!* New York: Gareth Stevens Publishing, 2014.

Dee, Willa. *Erosion and Weathering*. New York: PowerKids Press, 2014.

Walker, Kate. *Rocks*. New York: Cavendish Square Publishing, 2012.

Index

C
crust, 10, 14–15,
    20, 22

D
deforestation, 27

E
earthworms, 9
element(s), 4–5
erosion, 16

F
farmers, 12, 26
fossils, 18, 19

L
lava, 22

M
mineral, 15
mines, 21, 26

N
nutrients, 26

O
observation, 6

P
paper, 27
plant(s), 8, 14,
    18–19

R
rock(s), 14–16, 25
roots, 8

S
sand, 14, 16, 24
soil, 8, 13–14, 26
species, 23

W
wood, 27

Websites

For web resources related to the subject of this book, go to:
www.windmillbooks.com/weblinks and select this book's title.